HOW GENDER SPEAKS

SPEAKS

THOUGHT, WORD AND DEED

Cinthia Hiett, MC LPC

ISBN: 1533032963
ISBN-13: 978-1533032966

Contents

CHAPTER 1

Introduction

I always enjoy the discussion of gender differences in communication and how the opposite sex processes information and then speaks and acts as a result. It never ceases to amaze me how different the genders are, even though we are still human and share many characteristics. This discussion is not always welcome, however, in the academic arena. During my graduate work in the 90's, it was considered unethical and very unprofessional to talk about gender differences. It is very important to not confuse being *equal* with being the *same*. We are all equal as human beings, but we are simply not the same.

The following quote remarks on this ongoing tendency for us to throw away basic truths, thinking that we are evolving and progressing, only to re-visit them, pick them back up, and re-package them as original and new discoveries:

This is indicative of the thread that God weaves throughout history, which is undeniable and irreversible, as to the creation of His humans. We continue to revisit godly concepts, throw them away, only to pick them back up again. (Invisible War, Donald Grey Barnhouse[1])

One basic truth is that we are designed this way. The Bible states in the second chapter of Genesis that *it is not good for man to be alone.* This was not said, however, about women. Now this does not mean that it is not good for women to be in relationship. Women crave relationship.

What is continually astounding to me is that we get along at all! I am sure this is why man was created with such a desire for women, and women were created with a need to belong with and help men. Let's look at these simple truths:

Men are COMPELLED by a desire to be with women.

Women are COMPELLED by a desire or drive to help, complete, encourage, support, take care of, talk for, decide for, be wanted by, be desired by, and yes, to just *be* with a man.

Do you see the difference in even explaining the process? You see, innate in a man's desire is the need to protect, to cover, to be successful, and to be respected for those efforts. Very simple. It is not as complex for men as it is for women. Women are innately more complex, and if not handled appropriately, will complicate things, simply because of their hardwiring.

This does not mean that men are not complex! It means that men innately simplify things as a way to problem solve, and women complicate things because of all the feelings, experiences, and possibilities given in any moment, regardless of the inter-relational

We are made whole be being in relationship with one another.

activity.

Please understand that women don't necessarily complicate situations intentionally; much of the complication that occurs is a result of their attempt to clarify and resolve. If you don't understand this, you will treat them like a man and then get a very agitated, upset, hurt, unhappy, and VERY complicated woman.

One the other hand, if women don't understand the beauty of a man's simplicity, they will never be able to get their needs met and enjoy a life where things aren't so complicated. I am very thankful for my husband's simplicity especially in the face of conflict. For instance, if we have a difficult evening and I cannot successfully resolve an emotional moment (this is different than a moral/ethical moment which I teach women to distinguish between), he can wake up the next morning, and he is "fine." *Really*??! He sees it as a "bad moment," not a relational crisis that should result in seeing a therapist.

The beauty of gender interaction is in knowing how to take cues from each other regarding what things to tackle and what things to minimize. Just as in the case of the difficult evening I just mentioned, my husband saw the conflict as not a major "thing." We could then move on.

In my practice I deal with men in the arena of being overly optimistic, in that their tendency is to see each event as isolated and not connected to a pattern. This serves them well if they are taking on a nation in battle, or needing to commandeer an evening's meal. But if they are trying to be relational, they need to connect the dots! This is something men seldom want to do. I am so thankful that my husband forgets so many things about me.

Imagine for a moment if we were made exactly the same . . . first of all, no work would be ever accomplished if we had the same sex drive! And secondly, we would never be able to move on to the next moment because, to a woman, everything *means* something, and everything has to be processed and resolved or it stays in stasis waiting to be awakened at any moment.

All this to say: God obviously knew what he was doing when he created the masculine and feminine sides. We are made whole by being in relationship with one another. Please understand that I am not trying to make a doctrine out of this thought. I am simply trying to make a difficult, and sometimes painful, difference easier to assimilate.

Some simple truths about men:

- He does not wish to be questioned all the time about what or why he is doing what he is doing.
- He wants to be trusted implicitly.
- He wants support and trust for the way he does things.
- He doesn't want to explain his feelings. It's a more difficult neurological process to express/explain his feelings, and it creates intense vulnerability.
- He wants to be our hero, our protector, and our provision.

Some simple truths about women:

- She talks about how she feels.
- She feels BIG feelings and wants to be perceived correctly.
- She can really get her feelings hurt.
- She wants to be on the same page.
- She wants to reason together.
- She wants to connect and be intimate.
- She wants to be wanted and to be pursued.

We are made differently, but it is those

differences that make us uniquely and perfectly suited to be in relationship with one another, complementing and completing in perfect design.

CHAPTER 2

The Science behind Gender Differences

We have established that men and women have unique responses to environmental and relational stimuli. Why is this? Let's take a look at the epicenter of perception: the brain.

The Hardwiring of the Brain—both perceiving and receiving of information and experience.

Men have approximately 6.5 times more gray matter in the brain than women. But before the heads of all the men start to swell, listen to this: Women have about 10 times more white matter than men do.[2] This obvious contrast in white versus gray matter may account for differences in how men and women think.

Men seem to think with their gray matter, which is full of active neurons. Women think with the white matter, which consists more of connections between the neurons. In this way, a woman's brain is a bit more complicated in setup, but those connections may allow a woman's brain to work faster than a man's. [3]

The "defend your turf" area—dorsal pre-mammillary nucleus—is larger in the male brain and contains special circuits to detect territorial challenges by other males. And his amygdala, the alarm system for threats, fear, and danger, is also larger in men. These brain differences make men more alert than women to potential threats.

Meanwhile, the "I feel what you feel" part of the brain—mirror-neuron system—is larger and more active in the female brain. This enables women to naturally get in sync with others' emotions by reading facial expressions and interpreting tone of voice and other nonverbal emotional cues (i.e. what they pick up on at parties). Often, women assume that men have the same ability and end up hurt, disappointed, and sometimes angry. [4]

The male brain is also characterized by *systemizing* tendencies (to use Baron-Cohen's[5] term) and *mechanistic* thinking (to use Crespi and Badcock's[6] term). "Systemizing" is the drive to analyze, explore, and construct a system. The systemizer intuitively figures out how things work or extracts the underlying rules that govern the behavior of a system. The purpose of this is to understand and predict the system or to invent a new one.

In contrast, the female brain is characterized by *empathizing* tendencies (Baron-Cohen) or *mentalistic* thinking (Crespi and Badcock). "Empathizing" is the drive to identify another person's emotions and thoughts and to respond to them with an appropriate emotion. Empathizing occurs when we feel an appropriate emotional reaction in response to the other person's emotions. The purpose of this is to understand another person, to predict his or her behavior, and to connect or resonate with him or her emotionally.

The difference between "mechanism" and "mentalism" is similar to the difference between "systemizing" and "empathizing." In short, mechanism is about figuring things out (folk physics); mentalism is about understanding people (folk psychology). [7]

CHAPTER 3

How We Are Different

In the best-selling book *Men Are From Mars, Women are from Venus* by John Gray, Ph.D. the author looks at men and women as being either *centripetal* (pulling inward) or *centrifugal* (expansive).

Men are *Centripetal*:

    a. Men do not pick up on subtleness.

    b. Men are able to keep irrelevant information out.

    c. Danger-Pleasure: Men experience their environment as either dangerous or pleasurable (these are in constant flux).

    d. Happy-Mad: Men are either in a state of "happy" or "mad"—there is very little gray area.

e. Information and/or Experience: Men process everything in light of "How does it affect *me*?"

For example, at a party a woman notices all the subtle cues that are happening all around her. A girlfriend slams a tray down, an understated glance is exchanged between friends, or a coworker stands lonely in the corner. Women notice everything because they need to process their environment in order to relate to it.

On the other hand, men may not notice these subtle cues. And even if they do, they tend to just ignore it. This is how they are hardwired; it is what makes them good hunters. Men only take in information that is pertinent to what they are doing at that moment.

This may seem selfish, but there is a reason behind it: they feel a constant need to protect themselves from their environment. They are more than willing to die for a good cause (protecting those

Men only take in information that is pertinent to what they are doing at that moment.

they love). Men need to make sure they aren't going down because if they do, their whole kingdom is going down.

This is why men are so focused and may give terse responses when called during work. While women usually welcome interruptions as opportunity to engage with another person, men have to prioritize the sale they are negotiating (primary, determines livelihood) over the seemingly smaller issues that his wife may call with (still important to him, but secondary). This is why I tell my male clients to take a deep breath before answering a call from their wife and put their "nice voice" on before answering. Or, if in the middle of something critical, establish with their wife ahead of time that they will return her call as soon as possible.

Let me share a recent client story regarding the centripetal nature of men. A couple was preparing to send their daughter off to a very prestigious internship after her sophomore year in college. Both the husband and wife had noticed that their daughter had not packed much and did not seem very motivated to prepare herself. The husband shared how that made him angry. He just knew that his daughter would wait until the last minute to pack, which would leave him throwing belongings in his truck the morning of their long journey to her new city.

The wife, on the other hand, intuited that perhaps the daughter was feeling overwhelmed at the idea of the new job in the new city, far away from her hometown, parents, and everything that was comfortable to her. Perhaps her procrastination was linked to measuring up in the internship that was very competitive to acquire.

While the husband was thinking of himself and his ability to be successful with his daughter (facilitating the move), the wife was thinking about how the daughter was being affected by the move. At face value this makes the man look very selfish and the woman very caring. But what's really going on here is that he's thinking about how his daughter's behavior affects his ability to *help* her. He is getting more and more frustrated knowing that if his daughter does not do all of the concrete things that need to be done, he cannot make the trip work for her. He wants to be able to succeed *for* her.

The man was thinking in centripetal terms, and the woman was thinking more relationally. Once the wife shared her observations, the husband saw and understood more about the daughter's predicament, which helped him to relax and allow the process to occur.

Once we appreciate gender differences, we understand the different elements occurring within interpersonal interactions that are both equally relevant to the event. The man brings concrete action, while the woman brings emotional content. He brings "*what* we need to be doing," and she brings the "why."

Women are *Centrifugal:*

This is a force that tends to pull a thing outward—it is an *expansive* force. A woman's awareness moves out from her center. Her fundamental nature is to move out from herself and connect with others. The more deeply involved in relationships she becomes, the farther out she expands, and there is a tendency to lose herself in the process. In relationships, it is easy for her to become overwhelmed by the needs of others. Centrifugal nature is characterized by:

a. Difficulty compartmentalizing; our compartments bleed into one another.
b. Tendency toward rumination

    c. Taking in all information, can't keep it out (like "pop-ups" on a computer)

    d. Difficulty ignoring information (thinking about other tasks during sex)

    e. Information and/or Experience: Women process everything in light of "How does it affect *them*?"

Back to the story about the daughter moving away to her internship. While the husband thought in terms of *how is this going to affect me?* (packing truck last minute, etc.), the wife was trying to understand how the situation was affecting her daughter. She naturally was wired to see past the black and white of the situation into the needs of her daughter in order to *connect* with her. This is centrifugal thinking at its finest.

Another way to think of centripetal versus centrifugal thinking is with Windows...the computer version, that is! Think of men with only one window open at a time. Once one window is completed, he can then open a new window and complete that task. The term *one track mind* applies here. While men can work on multiple tasks quite efficiently, they are able to give their *full* attention to one thing at a time (work project, problem-solving, the football game, sex) and block out all distractions: centripetal.

Women, on the other hand, have several windows (or apps!) open simultaneously. They are constantly assessing what in their environment needs attention or evaluation and are easily drawn to other tasks while in the process of another. As they are not hardwired to compartmentalize everything like men, women tend to have different areas of their lives "bleed into" each other (home bleeds into work, work bleeds into home, etc.).

Fueled by a fundamental nature to move out from herself and connect with others, a woman is constantly taking in the information around her in an effort to understand and relate to her environment. Her brain is attempting to connect the dots to explain why an event is so relevant to her. Men's brains are hardwired to keep out any information not directly relevant to the task at hand (their brain does this for them, i.e. sex). A woman's brain, on the other hand, is designed to take in ALL the information and *then* decide what is relevant (and sometimes it *all* feels relevant!).

The Basic Needs of Men and Women

In her books, *For Women Only: What You Need to Know About the Inner Lives of Men* and *For Men Only: A Straightforward Guide to the Inner Lives of Women*,[8] Shaunti Feldhahn discusses the inner lives of both men and women as well as their basic needs. You guessed it—they are completely different.

Men need:

1. Respect
2. Success
3. Adventure/Challenge
4. Love of Beauty

Women need:

1. Security
2. Sense of Belonging, Being desired
3. Connectedness
4. Opportunity to express love (impact relationally)

"Rapport vs. Report" and "Relaters vs. Resolvers"

As a general rule, women talk to establish *rapport*, while men talk simply to *report*. The old saying, "Just the facts, ma'am," speaks to this dichotomy. Women are more relational with their conversation, which invariably leads to more words, while men just want the facts. As a result women can feel emotionally abandoned when men just say "okay" or look at them without a verbal response because women want *feedback*.

We can see a similar contrast when we look at how women talk in question form. Men interpret this as insecurity, wishy-washiness, a lack of confidence, and the need for help while women are looking for relational connection and a thoughtful response.

Let's look at this in a familiar scenario: a man and woman have just enjoyed a nice dinner out. On the way home, the woman says to the man, "My, that was a wonderful dinner, wasn't it?" She is looking to establish *rapport* and connect with her husband/boyfriend regarding the experience they just shared. More often than not, the man will reply with a simple, "Yes it was," without elaborating. This is because he talks to *report*. It's not that he isn't open to talking. Women may need to encourage conversation by asking questions directly related to the topic, thereby inspiring rapport.

Another generalization regarding gender

communication is that men are *resolvers* and focus on *doing*. The goal is to be *successful*. Women tend to be *relaters* who focus on *pleasing*. Communicating, connecting, understanding and being understood are the goals.

CHAPTER 4

Tips for Better Communication

If you want to be a better communicator, whether in relationship with your spouse, friends, coworkers, or employer, there are some tried-and-true methods that you can employ to ensure that you are making a connection effectively and not just causing conflict or confusion.

Improving Communication with Men

When communicating with men, it is very important to consider *affect*. This refers to how men perceive emotions and level of intensity. What happens when I am communicating anger, sadness, or hurt with them or another person? Men are easily unnerved by women's feelings. It is difficult for them to process a solution when it comes to emotions.

Tip #1: Discharge some of the intensity of emotion before talking with a man.

Why is this? Let me explain. Our brains are hardwired with a sympathetic nervous system response of *Fight, Flight, or Freeze*. When a woman comes to a man with a high intensity of emotion that he will not be easily able to process, his automatic, hard-wired response will be one of fight or flight. This can produce a great deal of stress and will not likely produce the kind of effective communication that women desire.

Look at what a man does, not what he says. What he DOES is what he means.

Because once a man feels attacked, he won't hear anything a woman says. When women are very upset, they should do the man in their lives a favor and speak with a girlfriend about their feelings first (without disrespecting the man).

Tip #2: Be careful to make your communication clear and as unclouded as possible with feelings that can be easily misunderstood.

When a woman is not managing her feelings well, it can make a man feel unsuccessful and disrespected—two of the needs of men discussed earlier. If women are not careful, the negativity in the expression of feelings can imply that a man is bad, irresponsible, or failing. Not only do men feel responsible for women's feelings, they are afraid, even terrified, of feelings.

Men are never sure where the feelings are going to go, how big they're going to get, and how to be successful with a woman feeling them. When women understand how uncomfortable with feelings men can be, they can help men be successful by clearly communicating their needs. When men say, "What do you want me to say?" simply *tell them* and appreciate when they do.

Once a man feels attacked, he won't hear anything a woman says.

Men need affirmation that they are not inherently bad. Look at what a man *does*, not what he says. *What he does is what he means.* In light of this fact, how should someone effectively express feelings with men? Non-verbal communication is very important.

Tip #3: Be mindful of your non-verbal communication.

It is important to be aware of facial expressions, tone of voice, body language, eye contact (different with subordinates), communicate only what is happening, and, finally, give them a way to succeed. The following non-verbal communication methods are interpreted differently by men and women.

- **_Head nodding:_** Women nod their heads to show that they are listening and engaged in the conversation, while men take it as agreement. Conversely, when men are listening, saying nothing, and have neutral body language, women interpret this as boredom, not understanding, or condescension.
- **_Smiling:_** Men smile to flirt, when feeling nervous, or when they are afraid. On the other hand, women smile to create rapport and/or a non-threatening environment.
- **_Eye contact:_** Women use this to create connection and relationship, while men use this to challenge and establish power.

- **Approach:** Women approach from the front, men approach from the side. Men interpret face to face interaction as personal or aggressive, while women see side interaction as showing disinterest or deception.

Tip #4: Talk in statements, not in question form.

As discussed earlier, men interpret communication in question form to be insecure, wishy-washy, and expressing a need for help. If you want to engage a man in conversation, avoid using questioning as a main tactic. When you ask a question, expect it to be answered as they are problem-solvers. "I want to be on the same page with you. Does that make sense to you? It is very important to me." Explain the problem and that it stresses you out. He will do anything to avoid conflict.

Tip #5: Be direct and avoid sarcasm.

As previously discussed, men are centripetal (inward-focused) versus women who are centrifugal (outward-focused). Men want to get to the point, while women want to express, understand, and "talk it out completely." In order to effectively communicate with a man, keep it focused and direct. Remember rapport vs. report? Keep your communication to talking in statements and more simple versus complex.

Tip #6: Give him a way to succeed in the communication.

Men have an innate need to be successful, so give him a way to succeed in the communication process and in *what* you are communicating about. Women seek to understand and be understood and want to protect the relationship, but to a man, success is more of an overlying goal.

Tip #7: R.E.A.P. Better Communication

R = Repeat and review what you hear him say.

E = Empathize with his feelings (or respect his feelings).

A = Acknowledge the validity of his message, even if you don't agree (this is respect).

P = Persist with patience until you can effectively communicate—eliminate defensiveness by controlling **affect** (how you are being perceived).

Improving Communication With Women

It's not as difficult as you may think. Validate and listen—this frequently solves the problem. Think of a visual example of an emotional "bell curve." A short version of this: When her feelings are escalating up that bell curve is when a man needs to *validate*. When she de-escalates, that is the time to *problem-solve*. When he validates as she escalates, she will naturally de-escalate because she will feel connected, and that will then give the opportunity to problem-solve if she needs it. Listening and validating more often than not "solves" the problem. A little sympathy goes a long way! Caring about a woman's feelings is an extremely powerful way to support and love a woman.

In fact, this is what women do for each other all the time. This is why it's amazing to men when they see women caring for each other:

Listen to what she says; don't look at what she does. What she SAYS is what she means.

"Nothing changed, but **everything** changed."

Consider the following:

> In an evening class at Stanford University the last lecture was on the mind-body connection—the relationship between stress and disease. The speaker, the head of psychiatry at Stanford, said that, among other things, one of the best things a man could do for his health is to be married to a woman, whereas one of the best things a woman could do for her health was to nurture her relationships with her girlfriends. At first everyone laughed, but he was serious.

> Women connect with each other differently and provide support systems that help each other to deal with stress and difficult life experiences. They share from their souls with their mothers, sisters, and friends. It turns out that this is very good for women's health. Physically, this quality "girl time" helps us to create more serotonin, a major neurotransmitter that helps combat depression and can create a general feeling of well-being.

> He said that spending time with a friend is just as important to our general health as exercise. Some think that jogging is healthy but time with friends is wasted. Not true. In fact, he said that failure to create and maintain quality relationships with other humans is as dangerous to our physical health as smoking! So the next

time you or a woman you love is spending time with a good friend, rest assured that they are practicing good health!

So what tips can you follow in order to improve communication with the women in your life?

Tip #1: Validate her feelings and really listen.

Women feel feelings all the time. They have also been learning how to handle them for a long time. For the most part, they really just *need* to feel them, and feel them *with* someone. When a woman says, "You're not listening," when you have been listening for the last 20 minutes, it usually means that you are not emotionally connecting with her, being compassionate, or being sympathetic.

Tip #2: Resist the urge to problem-solve.

Caution: Don't confuse or interpret emotional intensity or distress as an indication as to whether or not a woman needs physical help or problem-solving. The hardest thing for a man to discern is what event needs *sympathy* and what event needs *action*.

Tip #3: Err on the Side of Compassion.

Men can trust their instincts—if they don't know what to do or how to fix it, it's probably because it requires validation and compassion more than action. If they can think of an immediate concrete solution, then there probably is one. Just always err on compassion first. The men reading this are probably all dealing with highly-intelligent, accomplished women. They problem solve every day and are very good at networking to get what they need (i.e., "The oil needs changing," all the way to "My, I was misinterpreted, and now the whole group thinks 'blah, blah, blah' about me").

Tip #4: Don't get defensive.

It is natural for men to take on a defensive posture when past events are revisited. Realize that if she brings up the past, it isn't necessarily to rehash it. It is merely to explain how relevant the current situation is. Her brain creates reference points for how she establishes reality.

Her ability to remember has to do with the amount of estrogen in her brain. This hormone increases the amount of cortisol, a memory-boosting hormone produced by the adrenal gland during stressful moments, that makes those past events more easily retrievable. An example of this in women is the release of oxytocin after childbirth. If that biological process did not occur, she would never have a baby again because the memory would be too traumatizing. The level of oxytocin overrides the cortisol. When she is referring to something in the past, she does it to reiterate, confirm, refer to, or explain how she is currently feeling.

Tip #5: Relax.

Take a lot of deep breaths, purposefully relax your body. This calms down the sympathetic nervous system and helps you stay present while not having to "do" anything. There's a saying that the drunk driver always survives the crash. Remember the "3 B's": Broken **B**ones, Nobody's **Br**eathing, or **B**lood. That's when you HAVE to *do* something. If it's not dangerous, immoral, or unethical, relax. It's okay to just observe and care!

Tip #6: Meet her emotional needs first, THEN problem-solve.

When communicating with a woman it is important to enter into her emotional world *first* and then enter her intellectual world to problem solve. Do this by listening and validating. A man will have better access to a woman's intellectual world and physical world if they enter emotionally first (this is why women are more susceptible to the emotional manipulation of "womanizers").

Predictably, this is the opposite for men. If one wants to enter into their emotional world, they will have easier access if they first enter their intellectual or physical world.

Tip #7: Women LOVE information.

One of the greatest needs a woman has relationally is information. If a woman does not receive information, she will fill in the blanks. If a man knows that, he can set himself up to succeed so he has control over the way the information is presented. Resist seeing the giving of information as "answering to her" or feeling subordinate. Women need to appreciate the information they get from men knowing that it was given in the spirit of connecting with her on *her* level of emotional need.

How NOT to communicate with a woman:

1. Taking her emotions personally when she is venting and/or expressing feelings about someone or something else.

2. Being frustrated or angry because you are uncomfortable.

3. Trying to talk her "out" of how she feels or telling her she doesn't really need to feel that way and why (even though you are really trying to help).

4. Trying to understand her feelings through *your* world versus accepting them coming from *her* world. "Feelings are very real, but they are not always true."

Quick Tips for Communicating During an Argument:

Both: Use "I" statements ("I feel hurt" vs. "You are frustrating.")

Men:

o   Show her that you are hearing her concerns and value her feelings.

o   Don't ever tell a woman to calm down. This will just make the feelings escalate.

o   Take a moment to calm down if you need to.

o   Keep your volume of your voice in mind.

o   Even though you are not wired to "learn" people, the burden is on you to "learn" your wife/girlfriend.

Women:

- Don't make him the enemy.
- Speak rationally, and he will hear you. Some of men's greatest needs are respect and success—give them a way to achieve both during an argument.
- It is your responsibility to explain yourself with as little emotion as possible.
- If there is an occasion for him to problem-solve, let him do so. It will give him the opportunity to feel fulfilled and valued.
- Keep your facial *affect* neutral while communicating your concerns. Instead of furrowed brows and a frown, try smiling and raising eyebrows. Your encouraging demeanor can positively affect the conversation.

CHAPTER 5

Relationships and Gender Differences

It is no surprise that intimate relationships can be a hotbed of poor communication. As we have learned, we are created to process our environments and feelings very differently as men and women.

One thing I hear about a lot in my practice are the fears that men and women face as they head into the commitment of marriage. Women wonder, "Is he going to continue to be the man that I dated, the man that pursued me with a vengeance and made everything perfect? Will I be okay? What will become of me? Who will I become?"

Men, on the other hand, wonder, "Will I be put in a box, will I be confined, and lose all my independence? Will I not be able to explore, to stretch, to challenge myself, to make mistakes, to live? Will my wings be "clipped"? Is my life over?"

Looking at it from the point of view of the opposite sex, a man or woman's fears may seem either valid or unfounded, but they are very real. Understanding where your spouse is coming from is crucial to understanding them as a person.

It is often said that communication is the key to a good marriage. This is very true. I have no doubt that you have had some "light bulb" moments as you have read through this communication guide. The real challenge is putting all of these tips into practice despite the years and years of doing it the "wrong" way.

CHAPTER 6

Closing Thoughts

Accepting Our Gender Differences

Bottom line? The biggest takeaway about gender is to not take it personally. It's hard to not take it personally. But we were created to be in relationship with one another. Achieving this on a more practical level begins with true acceptance and appreciation of one's unique personhood. This is profoundly healing and has an exponential effect on intimacy.

One of the most difficult aspects of relating in a healthy manner (which is the only way to produce true intimacy) is determining "what" to accept as one's true identity. The ability to determine "who" the authentic person is in order to truly accept, know, and support the individual directly correlates with understanding the difference between gender, temperament, and dysfunction. It is so important to understand gender while not making gender differences an excuse to behave in one way. Gender and temperament are God-given and need complete acceptance. Dysfunction, on the other hand, steals one's true identity and must be changed.

> *True relationship begins with a genuine acceptance and appreciation of one's unique personhood.*

Dr. Gray's book, *Men are from Mars, Women are from Venus,* states the following: "The key to successful relationship between men and women lies in accepting our differences. That only through respecting, appreciating, and responding to our natural differences can we achieve real happiness."[9] I would take it one step further: we need to "love" the differences, "rejoice" in the differences, and be "fascinated" by the differences. Relationship between men and women was established as a way to further our intimacy, our understanding, and our appreciation of our Creator. Understanding, experiencing, and accepting the opposite gender enhances one's immediate relationships and those with the human community at large. We need to love our opposite, even if though it is different.

About the Author

Cinthia Hiett has been practicing as a licensed psychotherapist for the past twenty-six years, specializing in relationships, personality inventories, and image consulting. In addition to her thriving practice, Cinthia is a radio show personality and sought-after speaker who uses music, humor, and personal stories to make the concepts of communication and relationships come alive for her audience. She has presented numerous motivational seminars and has lectured on a variety of relationship, inspirational, and mental health topics.

Cinthia is known for her deep levels of expertise in relationships and helping individuals and couples learn new and different ways to have successful relationships. Both in her practice and speaking engagements, she introduces how thoughts, words, and actions create interpersonal success and connection or conflict and confusion. She explains how the power of words, tone, and nonverbal communication as it relates to gender differences. She helps clients and audiences discover tools and insights they can immediately begin using to improve communication with significant others, family, bosses, colleagues, or staff members.

Through her public ministry on the radio and in podcasts, Cinthia works to meet the needs of all listeners, whether they need support in an already healthy relationship, simply need help getting back on track, or require therapeutic intervention. Her messages are a way for her to extend her reach further into the community than her practice allows. She truly believes that if people had in their arsenal some basic information about relationships and communication, they wouldn't need therapy.

When people understand how to do relationships better and more effectively, their ministry becomes more effective as a result. When colleagues understand interpersonal relationship, there is less conflict in a business setting and more peace in the workplace.

Whether speaking to women in Africa or executives locally, the principles she teaches are revolutionary and life changing. Cinthia is available to speak to organizational or church staff, women's groups, men's groups, marriage conferences, and beyond. In fact, coaching and consultation for organizations and corporations are among her specialties. She helps teams of employees resolve conflict and learn to work more productively together, teaching them to manage the personalities and group dynamics present within a wide variety of employee/employer interactions.

Cinthia is available for private and corporate coaching, and for group and individual consulting sessions. Whether you need a motivational keynote about relationships and gender, an inspirational performance, or coaching/consulting for yourself or others, Cinthia brings a wealth of expertise, talent, and interest. With many years in the industry along with award-winning recommendations and testimonials, your next event or consultation with Cinthia will exceed your expectations!

Please visit www.cinthiahiett.com for more information.

Citations

1. Barnhouse, Donald Grey. 1965. *The Invisible War*. Grand Rapids, MI: Zondervan.
2. Carey, Bjorn. "Men and Women Really Do Think Differently." Live Science. How Stuff Works. January 20, 2005.
    http://www.howstuffworks.com/framed.htm?parent=men-women-different-brains.htm&url=http%3A%2F%2Fwww.livescience.com%2Fhealth%2F050120_brain_sex.html.
3. Hotz, Robert Lee. "Deep, Dark Secrets of His and Her Brains." How Stuff Works. Los Angeles Times, June 16, 2005.
    http://www.howstuffworks.com/framed.htm?parent=men-women-different-brains.htm&url=http%3A%2F%2Fwww.latimes.com%2Fnews%2Fscience%2Fla-sci-brainsex16jun16%2C0%2C5806592%2Cfull.story.
4. Brizendine, Louann. "Love, Sex, and the Male Brain." March 23, 2010, Special to CNN.
5. "Empathizing-Systemizing Theory." *Wikipedia*. Last updated March 18, 2014.
    http://en.wikipedia.org/wiki/Empathizing%E2%80%93systemizing_theory.
6. Badcock, Christopher. "The Imprinted Brain Theory." November 19, 2008. http://edge.org/conversation/the-imprinted-brain-theory.
7. Kanazawa, Satoshi. "A Look at the Hard Truths About Human Nature." *The Scientific Fundamentalist*.
8. Feldhahn, Shaunti. Paraphrased from *For Women Only: What You Need to Know About the Inner Lives of Men*, 2006, Multnomah Publishers; and *For Men Only: A Straightforward Guide to the Inner Lives of Women*, 2004: Multnomah Publishers.
9. Gray, John Ph.D. 1992. *Men Are From Mars, Women Are From Venus: the Classic Guide to Understanding the Opposite Sex*. New York, NY: HarperCollins Publishers.

33699036R00034

Made in the USA
San Bernardino, CA
08 May 2016